AF413619

HOW ARE MUMMIES MADE?

ARCHAEOLOGY QUICK GUIDE
CHILDREN'S ARCHAEOLOGY BOOKS

Speedy Publishing LLC

40 E. Main St. #1156

Newark, DE 19711

www.speedypublishing.com

Copyright 2017

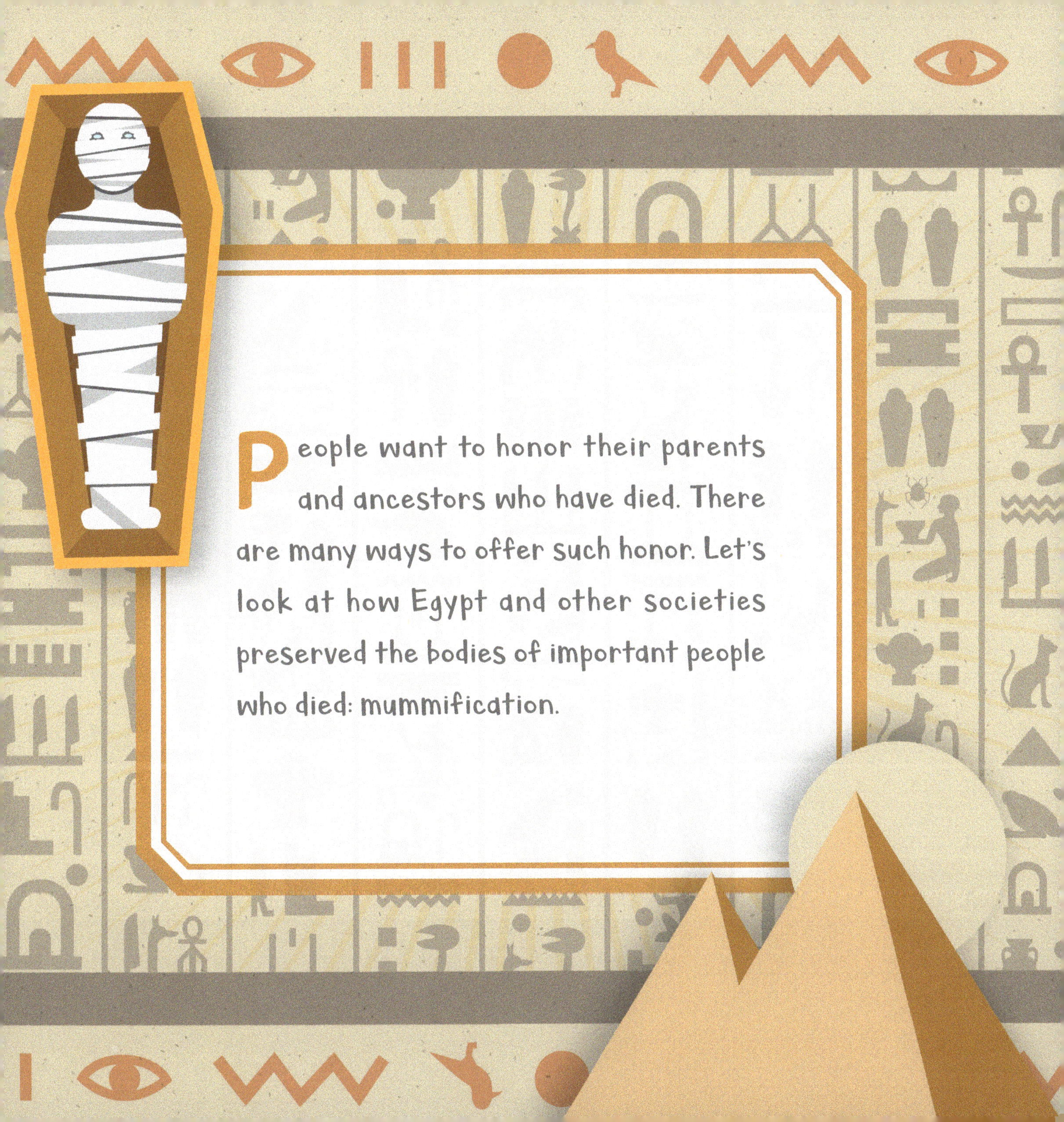

eople want to honor their parents and ancestors who have died. There are many ways to offer such honor. Let's look at how Egypt and other societies preserved the bodies of important people who died: mummification.

HONORING THE DEAD

When people we love die, we want to honor their memory. In some societies, though, people wanted to do more. The cultures of Egypt and many other lands believed that the end of this life was the start of life in a new world—and that the person moving to the new life would need a body to live in. So it was important to preserve the dead person's body.

EGYPT

EGYPTIAN MUMMY

THE EGYPTIAN WAY

Egyptians believed that five forces lived together in a person's body. The three most important were the ba and ka (like our concept of the soul), and the akh, the person's life in the next world. Egyptians believed that, after a person died in this world, the ba and ka would carry them into akh—but only if their body was available. So preserving bodies of people was very important in Egypt.

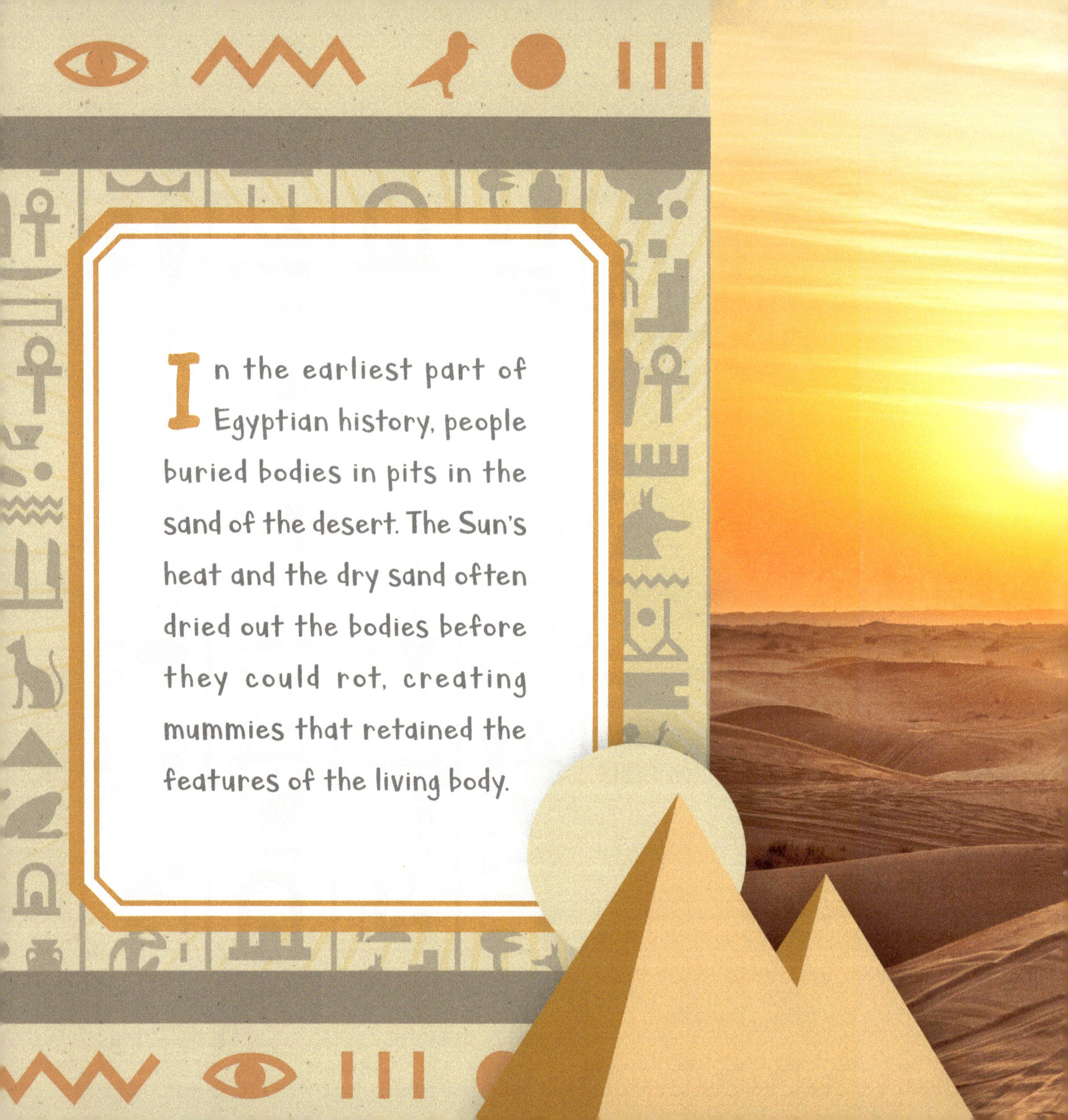

In the earliest part of Egyptian history, people buried bodies in pits in the sand of the desert. The Sun's heat and the dry sand often dried out the bodies before they could rot, creating mummies that retained the features of the living body.

EGYPTIAN DESERT

However, sometimes animals would find the bodies before they were dried out. To avoid this, the Egyptians started burying bodies in coffins. But then they found that bodies in coffins, protected from the heat of the sun, would decay, and this would defeat the goal of keeping the person's body available for use in the next world. So they developed ways of preserving the bodies so they would continue to look lifelike. This process is called mummification.

MUMMIFICATION

MUMMIFIED CAT

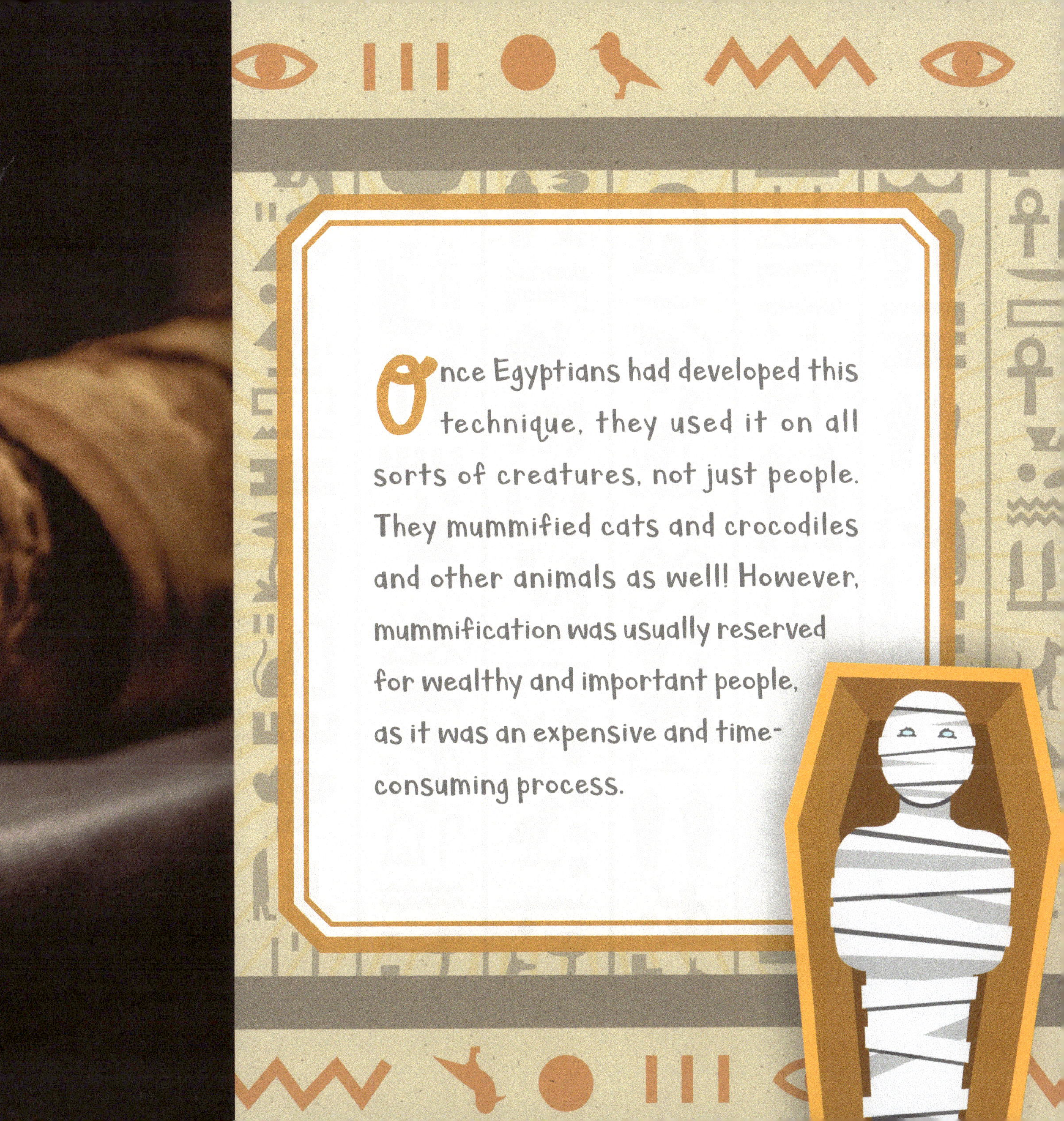

Once Egyptians had developed this technique, they used it on all sorts of creatures, not just people. They mummified cats and crocodiles and other animals as well! However, mummification was usually reserved for wealthy and important people, as it was an expensive and time-consuming process.

MAKING A
MUMMY,
STEP BY STEP

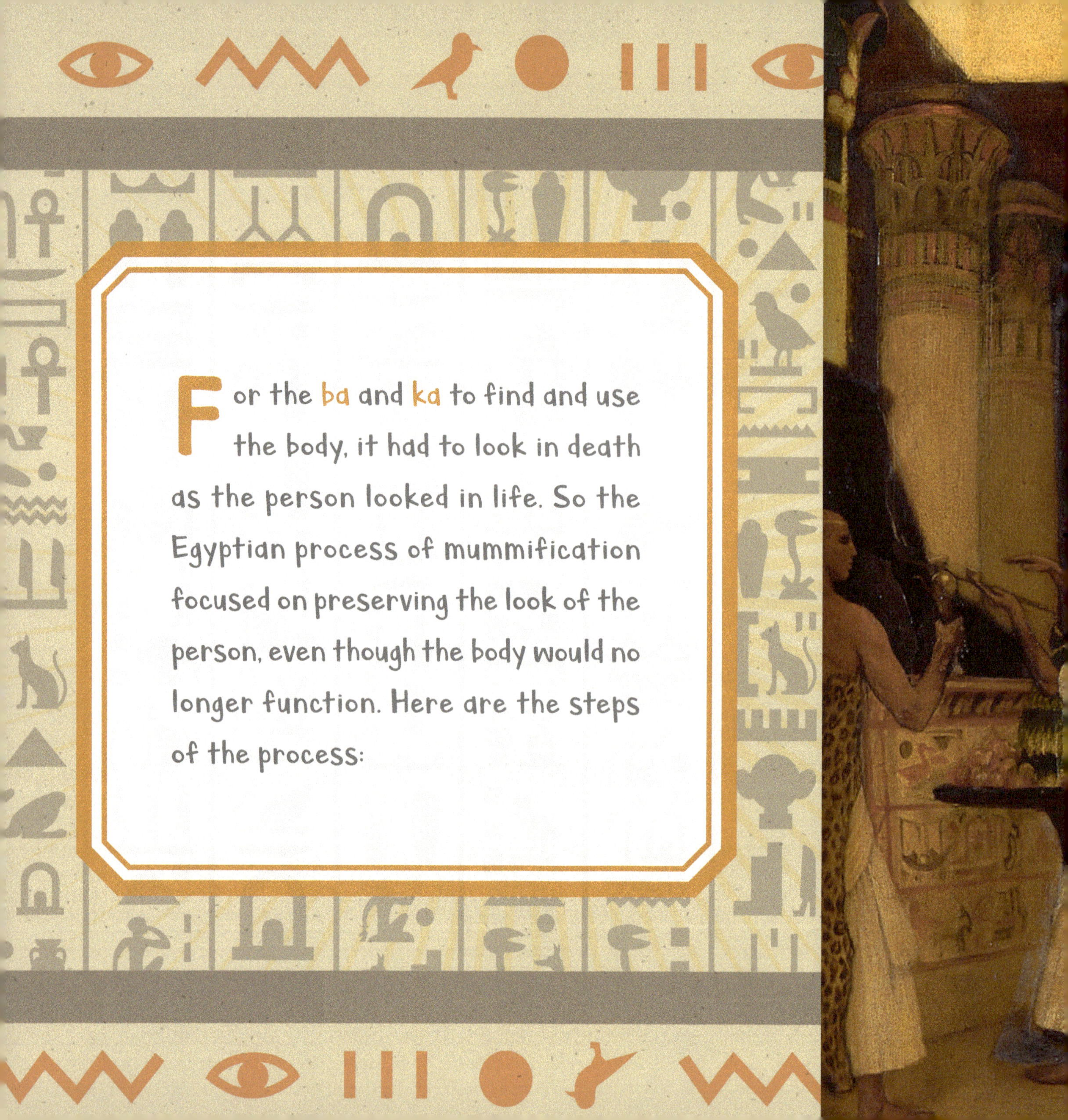

For the ba and ka to find and use the body, it had to look in death as the person looked in life. So the Egyptian process of mummification focused on preserving the look of the person, even though the body would no longer function. Here are the steps of the process:

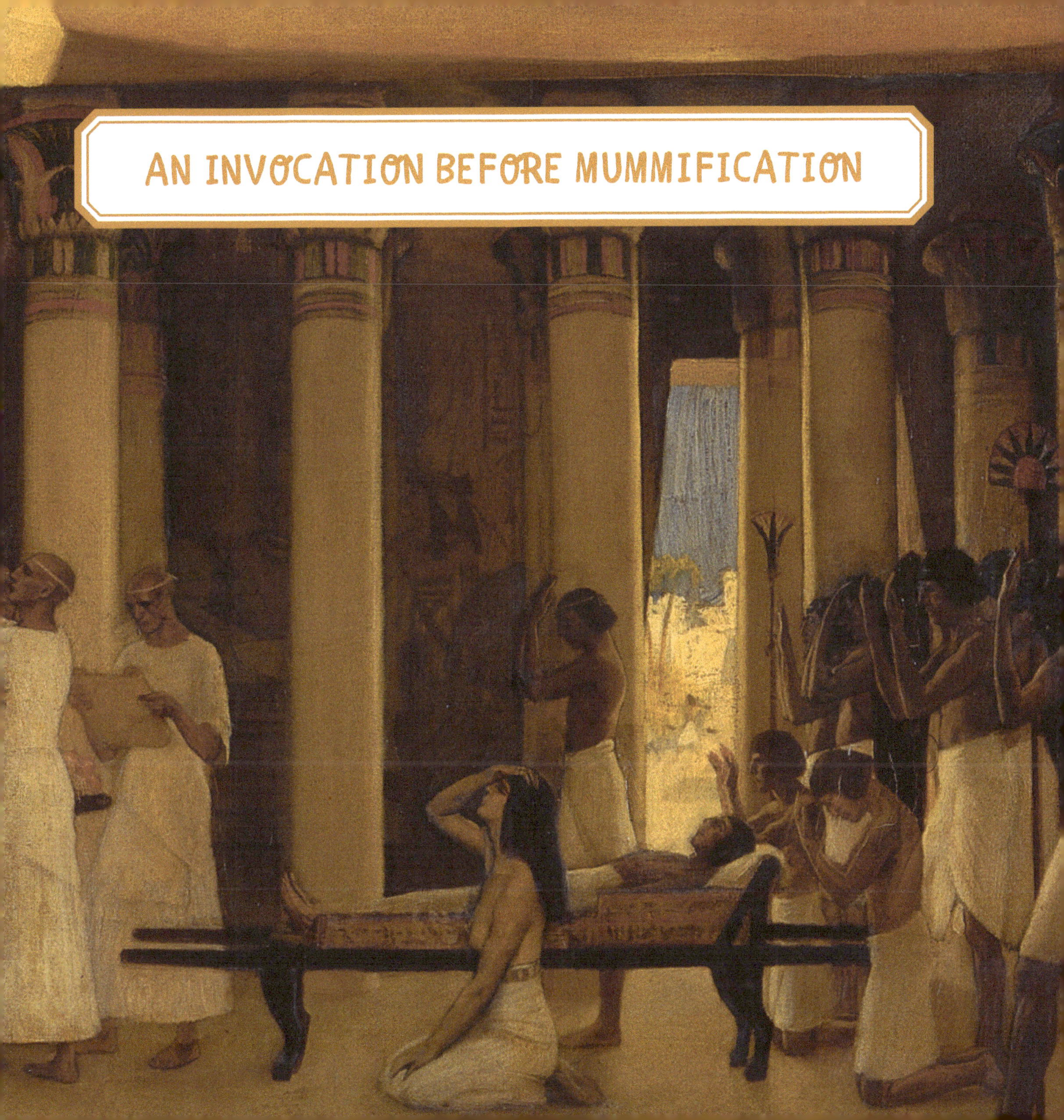

AN INVOCATION BEFORE MUMMIFICATION

SUNSET OVER NILE RIVER

Bring the body to the embalmer's tent on the west side of the Nile River. The west side is related to where the Sun goes down, or "dies", at the end of the day.

The chief embalmer would do his work wearing a mask of Anubis, the god of the dead.

Wash the body with a solution of salty water.

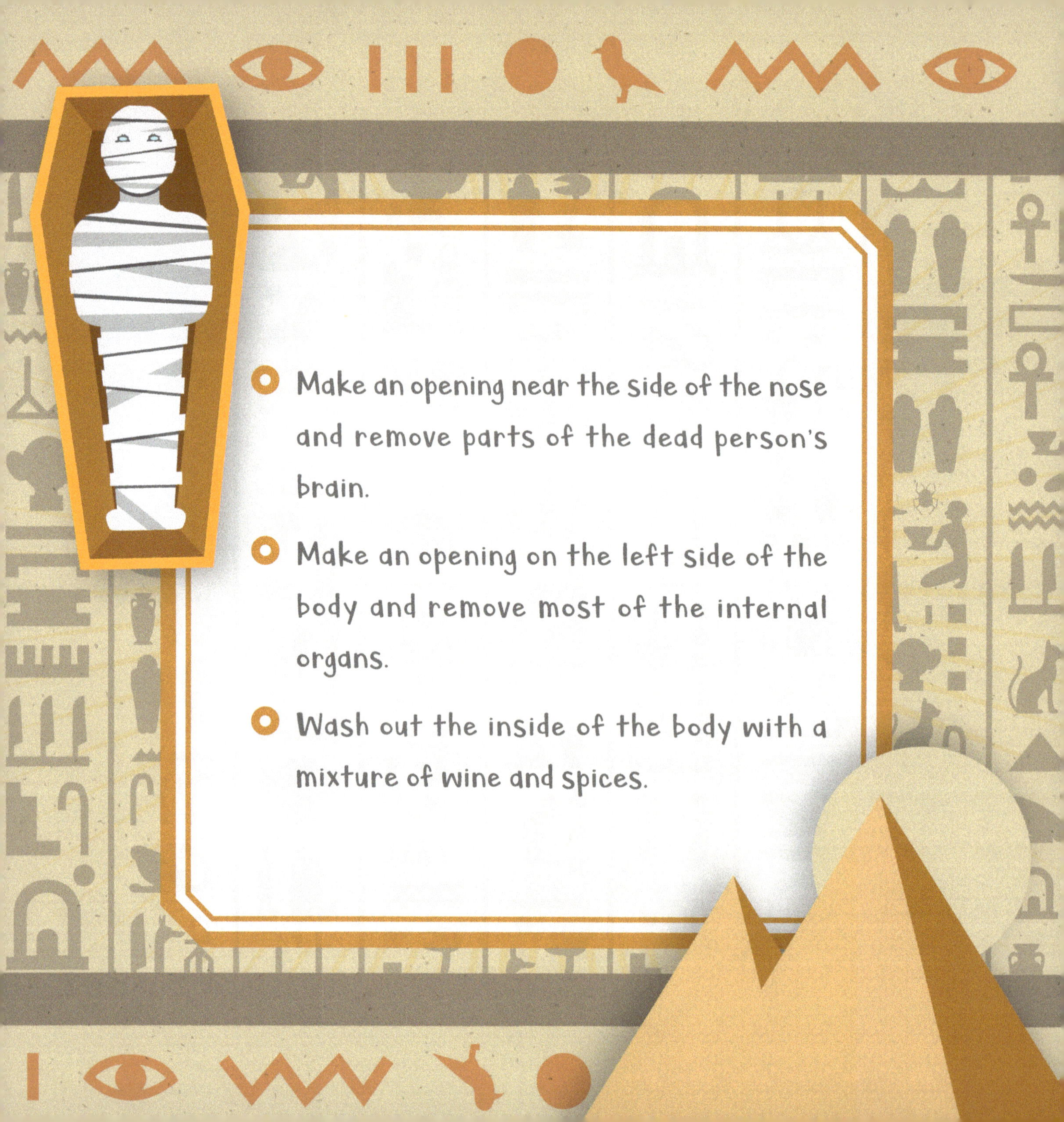

Make an opening near the side of the nose and remove parts of the dead person's brain.

Make an opening on the left side of the body and remove most of the internal organs.

Wash out the inside of the body with a mixture of wine and spices.

NATRON
FOUR STEP MUMMIFICATION

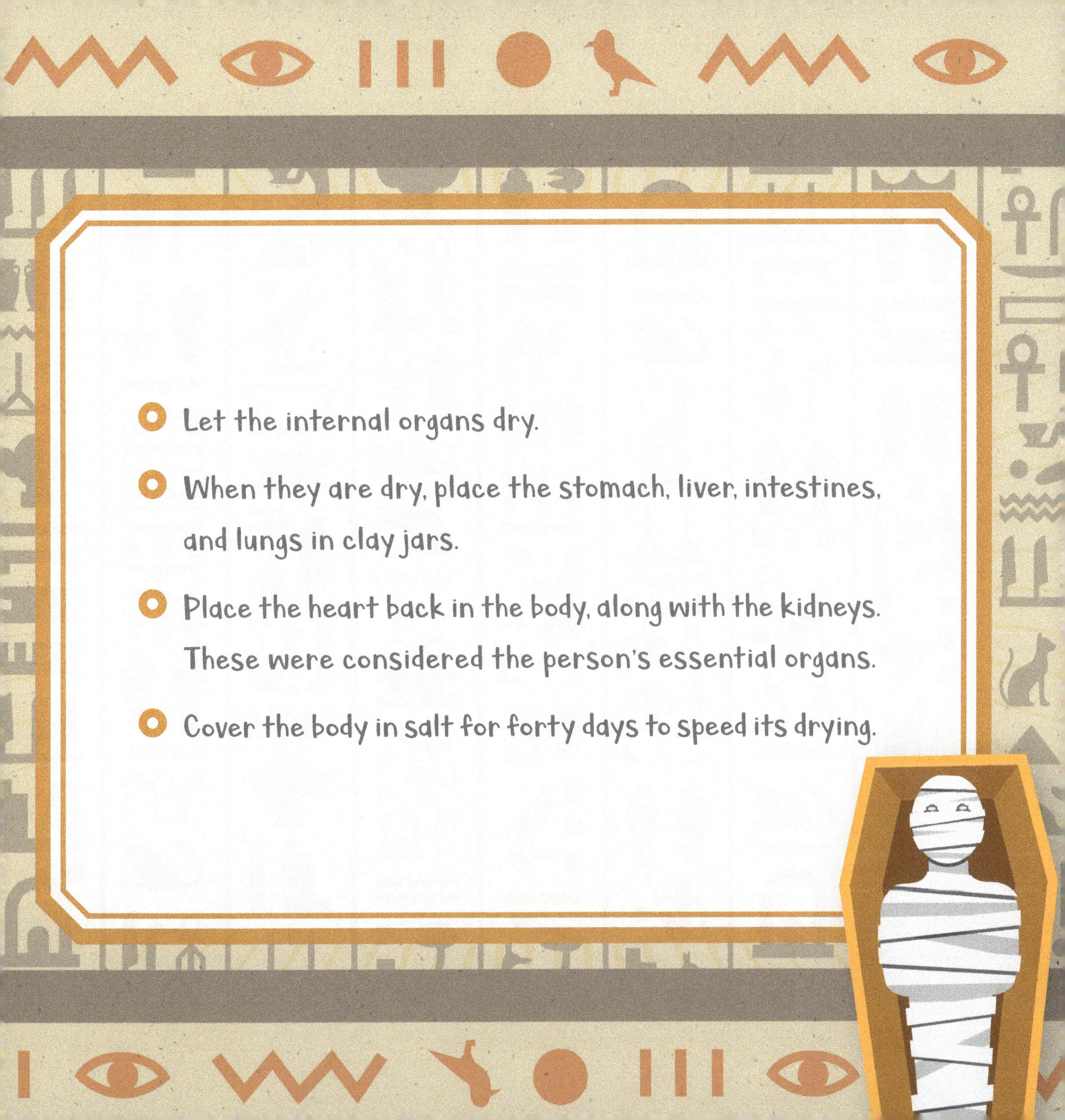

- Let the internal organs dry.

- When they are dry, place the stomach, liver, intestines, and lungs in clay jars.

- Place the heart back in the body, along with the kidneys. These were considered the person's essential organs.

- Cover the body in salt for forty days to speed its drying.

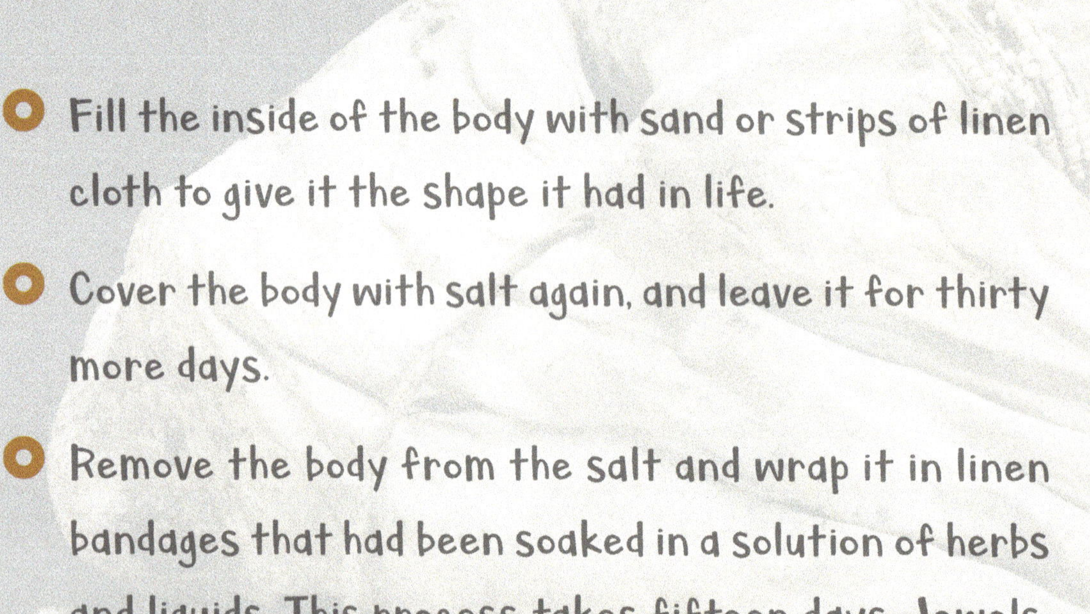

- Fill the inside of the body with sand or strips of linen cloth to give it the shape it had in life.

- Cover the body with salt again, and leave it for thirty more days.

- Remove the body from the salt and wrap it in linen bandages that had been soaked in a solution of herbs and liquids. This process takes fifteen days. Jewels, symbols of power and office, and other small items might be added at this stage. Pharaoh Tutankhamen's mummy had over 140 items included in its wrappings.

MUMMIFIED MALE BODY

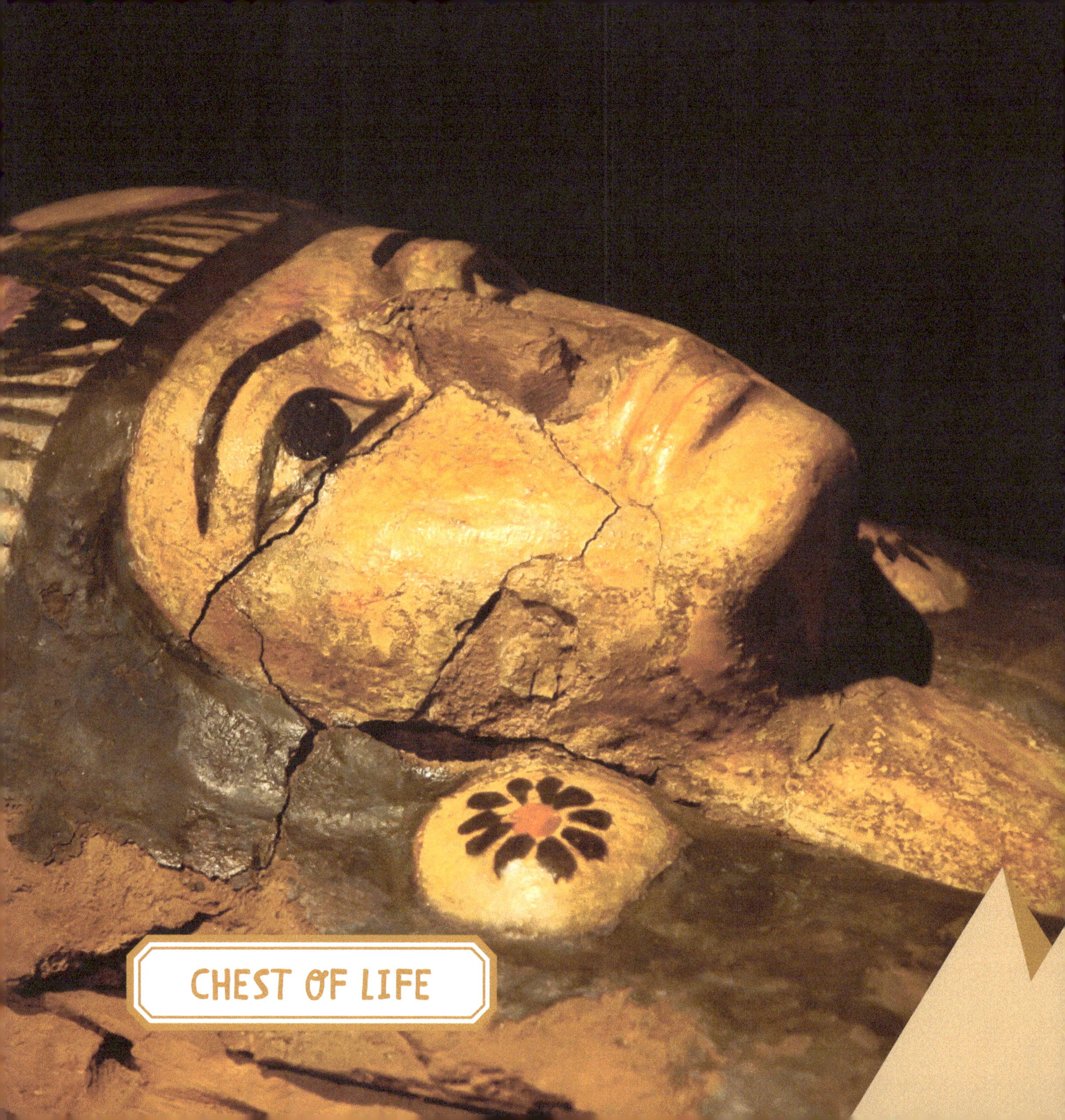

CHEST OF LIFE

CARING FOR MUMMIES

When the mummy was ready, it was placed in a "chest of life", an elaborate coffin. Sometimes these coffins were carved, painted, and decorated to look like the mummified person within, as that person had looked in the prime of life. There would be spells and prayers written on the coffin, and Egyptians believe that if, somehow, the mummy became lost, the coffin could act as a substitute that could carry the person's ba and ka into the akh.

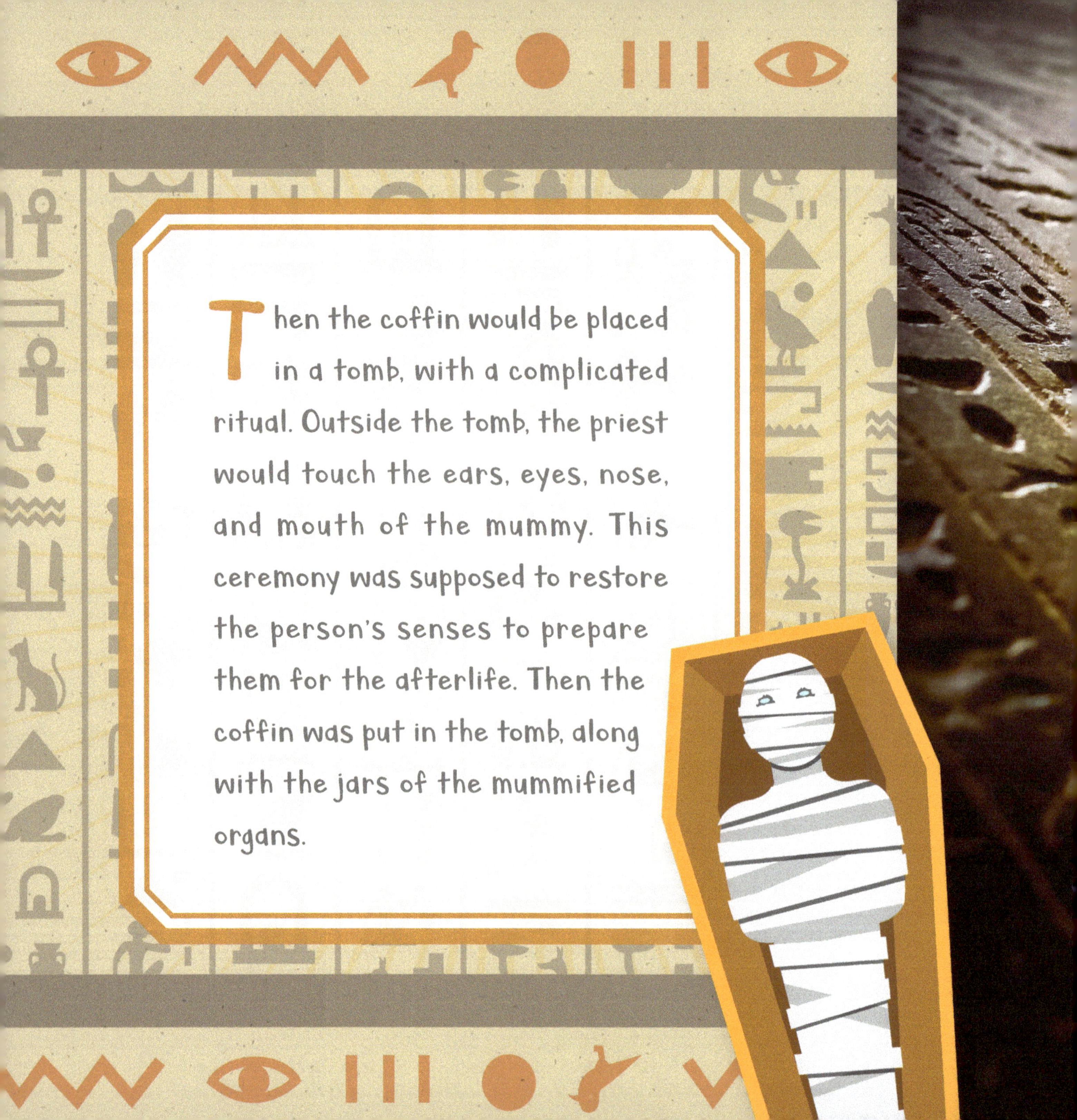

T hen the coffin would be placed in a tomb, with a complicated ritual. Outside the tomb, the priest would touch the ears, eyes, nose, and mouth of the mummy. This ceremony was supposed to restore the person's senses to prepare them for the afterlife. Then the coffin was put in the tomb, along with the jars of the mummified organs.

EGYPTIAN SYMBOLS
ON COFFIN

RAMESSES VI TOMB

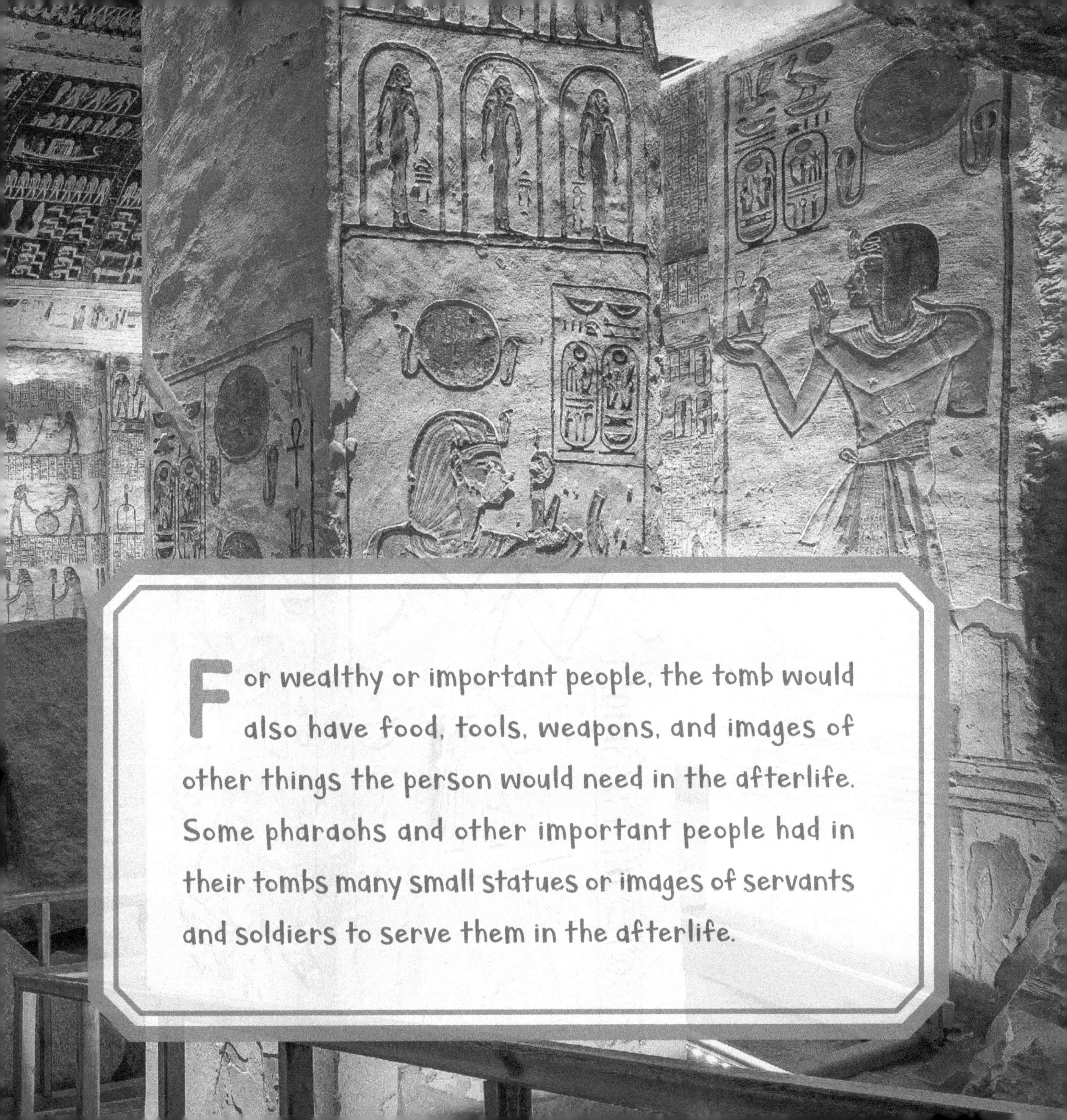

For wealthy or important people, the tomb would also have food, tools, weapons, and images of other things the person would need in the afterlife. Some pharaohs and other important people had in their tombs many small statues or images of servants and soldiers to serve them in the afterlife.

For the mighty and powerful, the tomb for the mummified body might be a pyramid. Others were buried in less-imposing structures.

GREAT PYRAMIDS OF GIZA

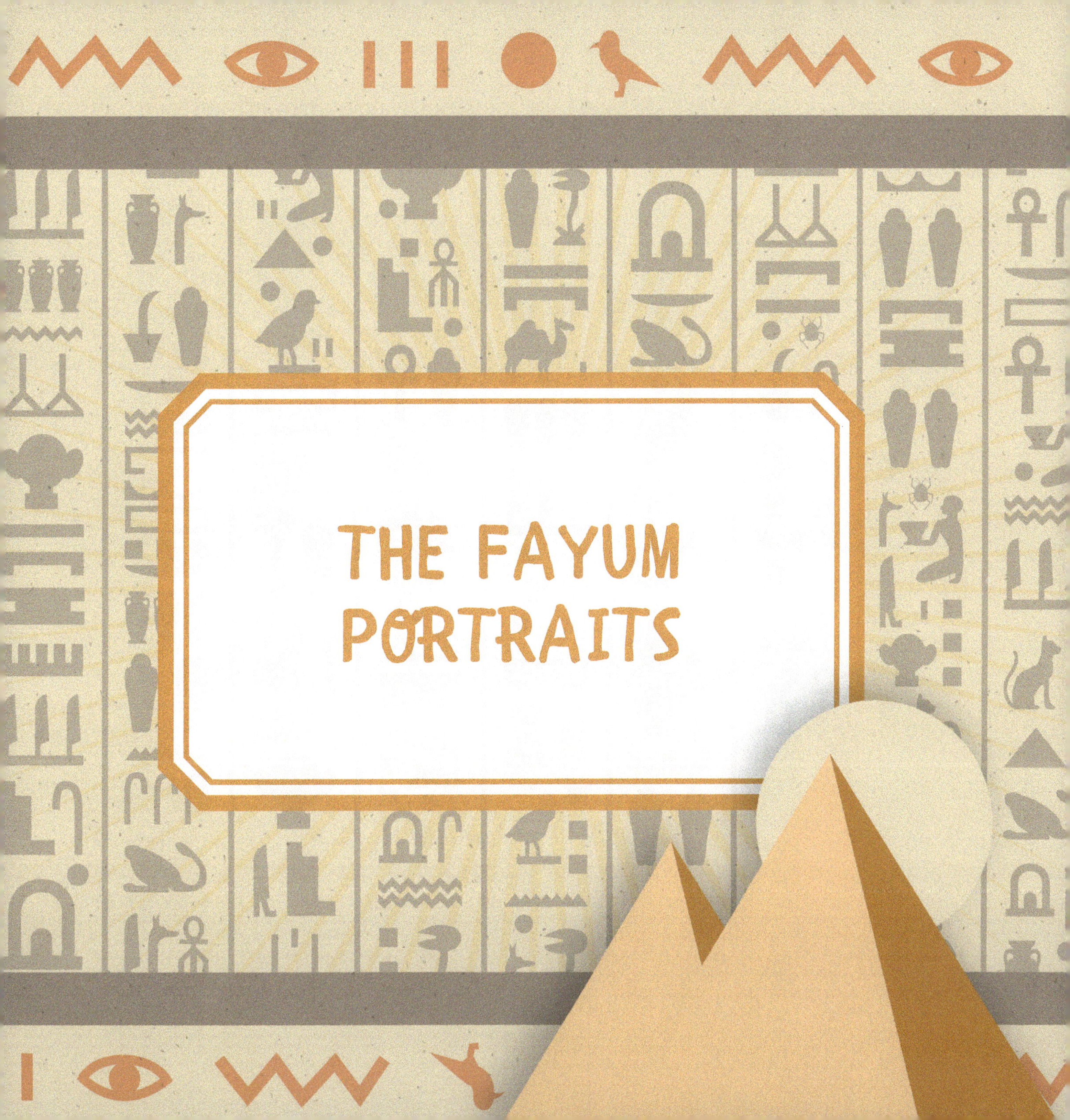

THE FAYUM
PORTRAITS

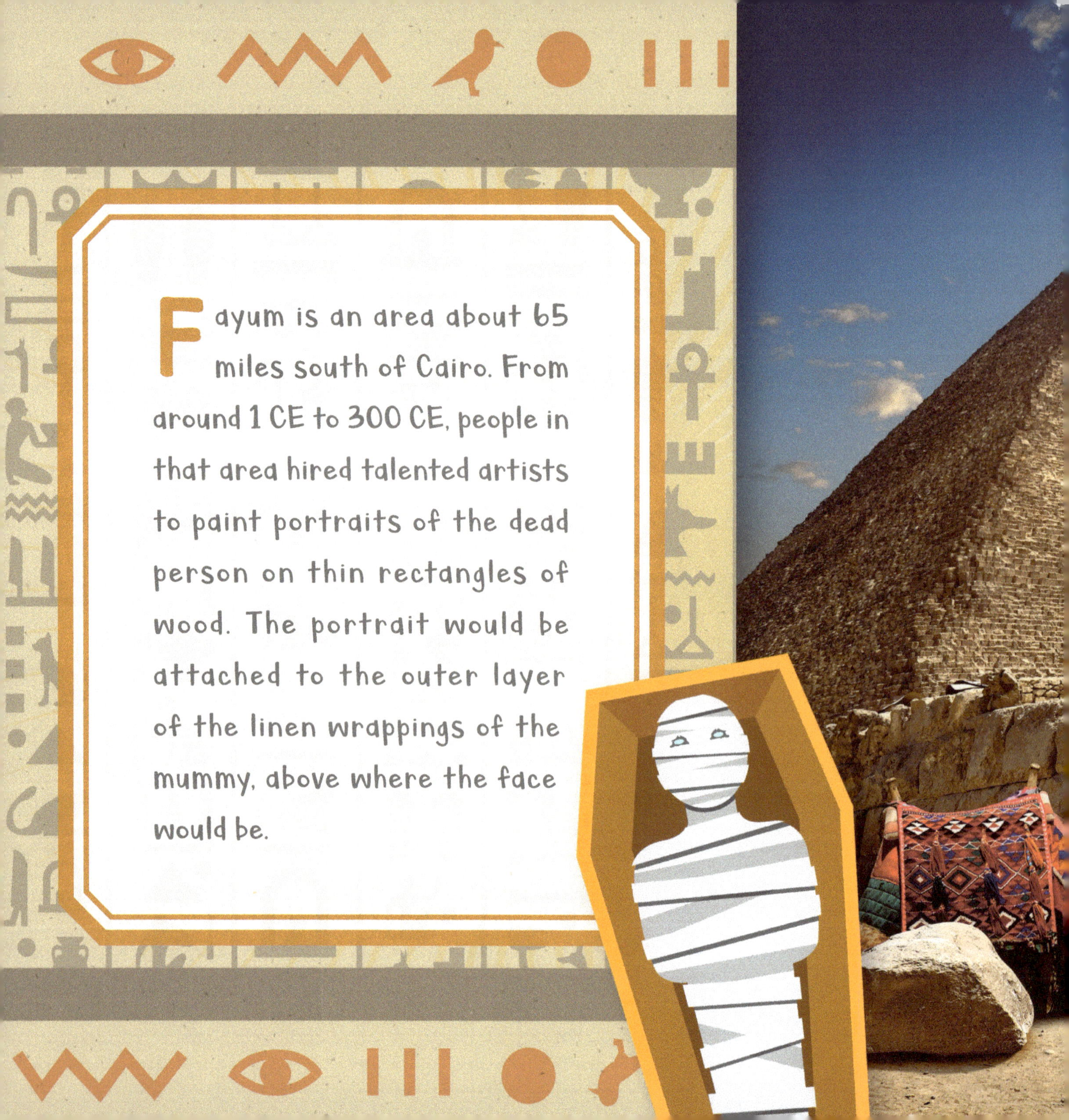

Fayum is an area about 65 miles south of Cairo. From around 1 CE to 300 CE, people in that area hired talented artists to paint portraits of the dead person on thin rectangles of wood. The portrait would be attached to the outer layer of the linen wrappings of the mummy, above where the face would be.

CAIRO

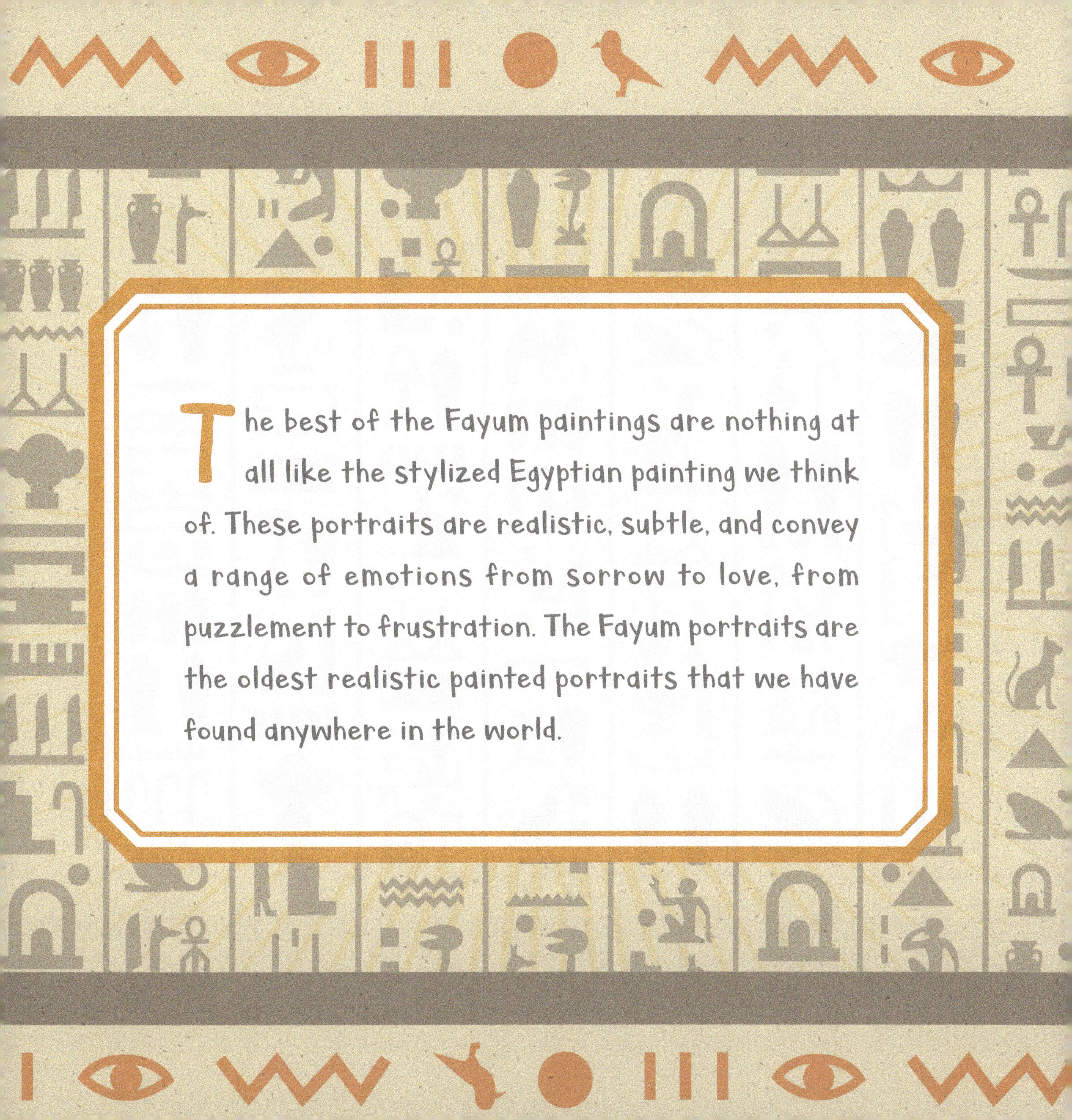

The best of the Fayum paintings are nothing at all like the stylized Egyptian painting we think of. These portraits are realistic, subtle, and convey a range of emotions from sorrow to love, from puzzlement to frustration. The Fayum portraits are the oldest realistic painted portraits that we have found anywhere in the world.

MUMMIES IN OTHER LANDS

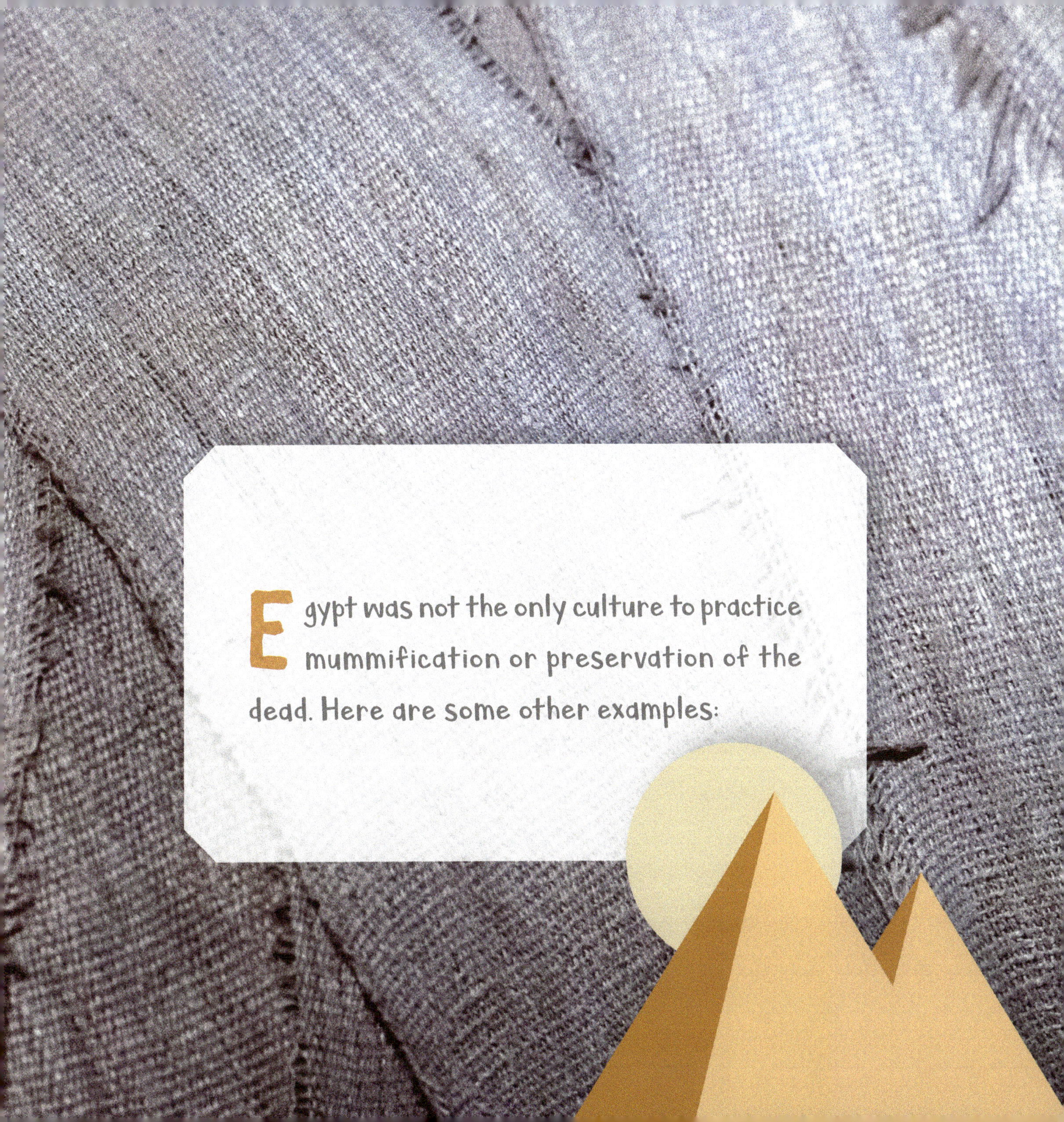

E gypt was not the only culture to practice mummification or preservation of the dead. Here are some other examples:

SOUTH AMERICA

The Atacama desert is high above the Pacific coast of Chile and Peru. There the Chinchorro people created the oldest mummies in the world, some dating from 6,000 BCE. The culture did not develop farming, pottery, woven cloth or a written language, but they had a complex series of techniques to honor and preserve the bodies of the dead.

BRA
BOLIVIA
LA PAZ
Cochabamba
SUCRE
Santa Cruz
Cuiabá
PARAGUAY
Paraguay
Campo
Grande
Go
Salta
Pilcomayo
Paraná
Antofagasta
ricorno
Tucumán
ASUNCIÓN
Ciudad
del Este
Cascate
dell'Iguaçu
San
ARGENTINA
Corrientes
Posadas
Cur
rdoba
Uruguay
Santa Fe
Parana
Santa Maria
Rosario
Luis
Flori
ENOS AIRES
Melo
Pôrto Aleg
URUGU

CHINCHORRO BANKS

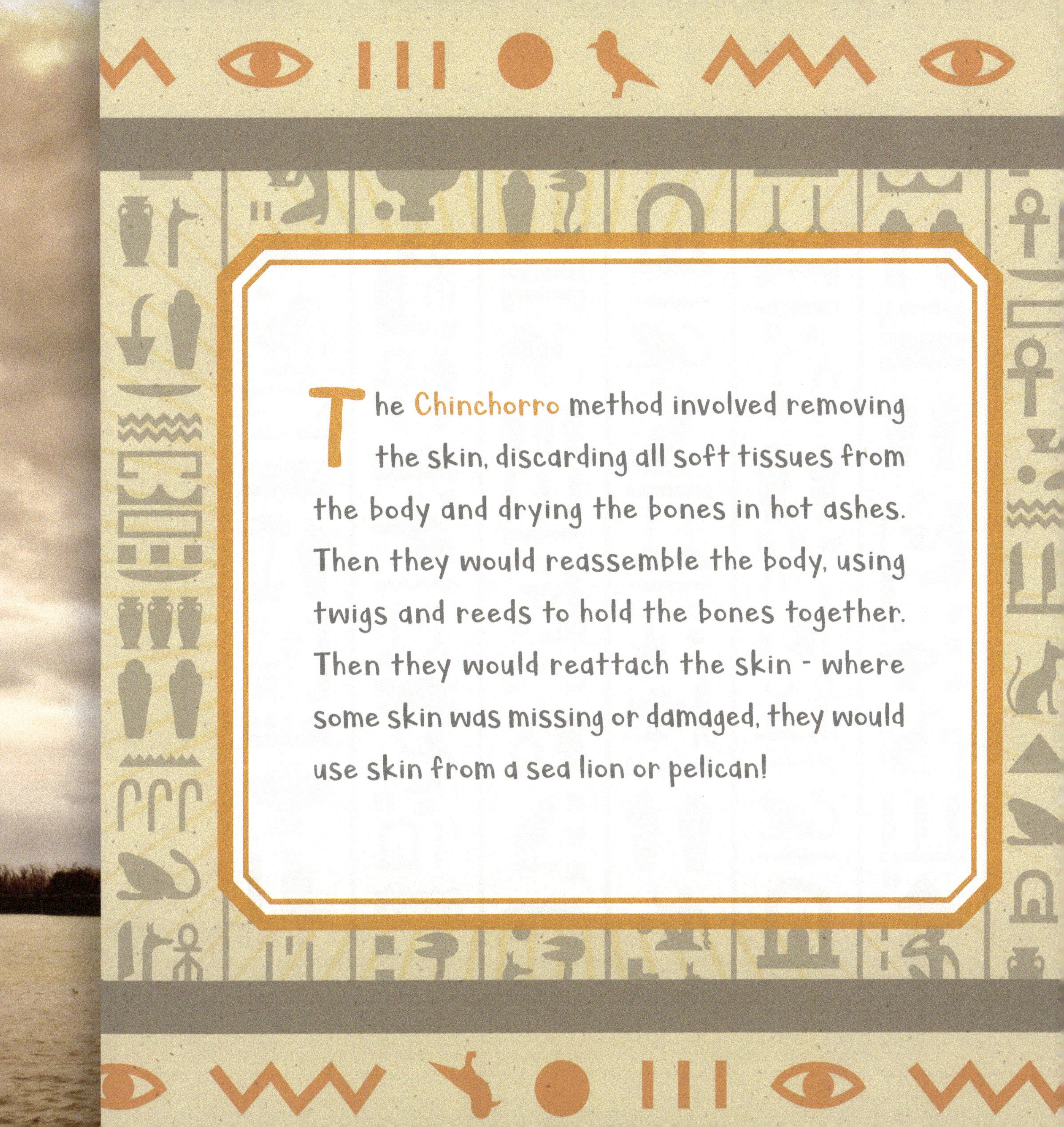

The Chinchorro method involved removing the skin, discarding all soft tissues from the body and drying the bones in hot ashes. Then they would reassemble the body, using twigs and reeds to hold the bones together. Then they would reattach the skin - where some skin was missing or damaged, they would use skin from a sea lion or pelican!

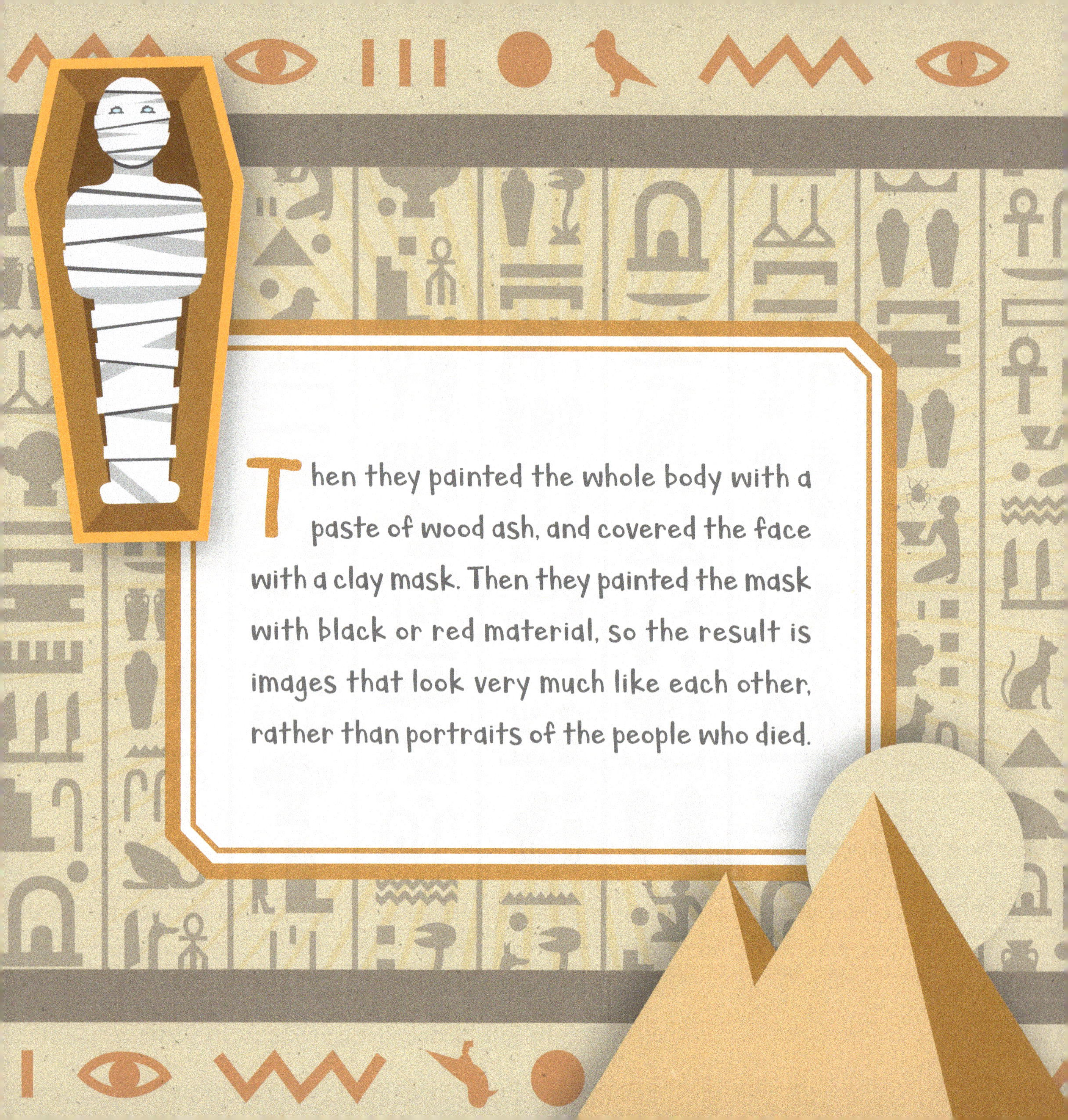

hen they painted the whole body with a paste of wood ash, and covered the face with a clay mask. Then they painted the mask with black or red material, so the result is images that look very much like each other, rather than portraits of the people who died.

CHINCHORRO MUMMY

The mummies were buried in family groups, including the mummies of children who had died young.

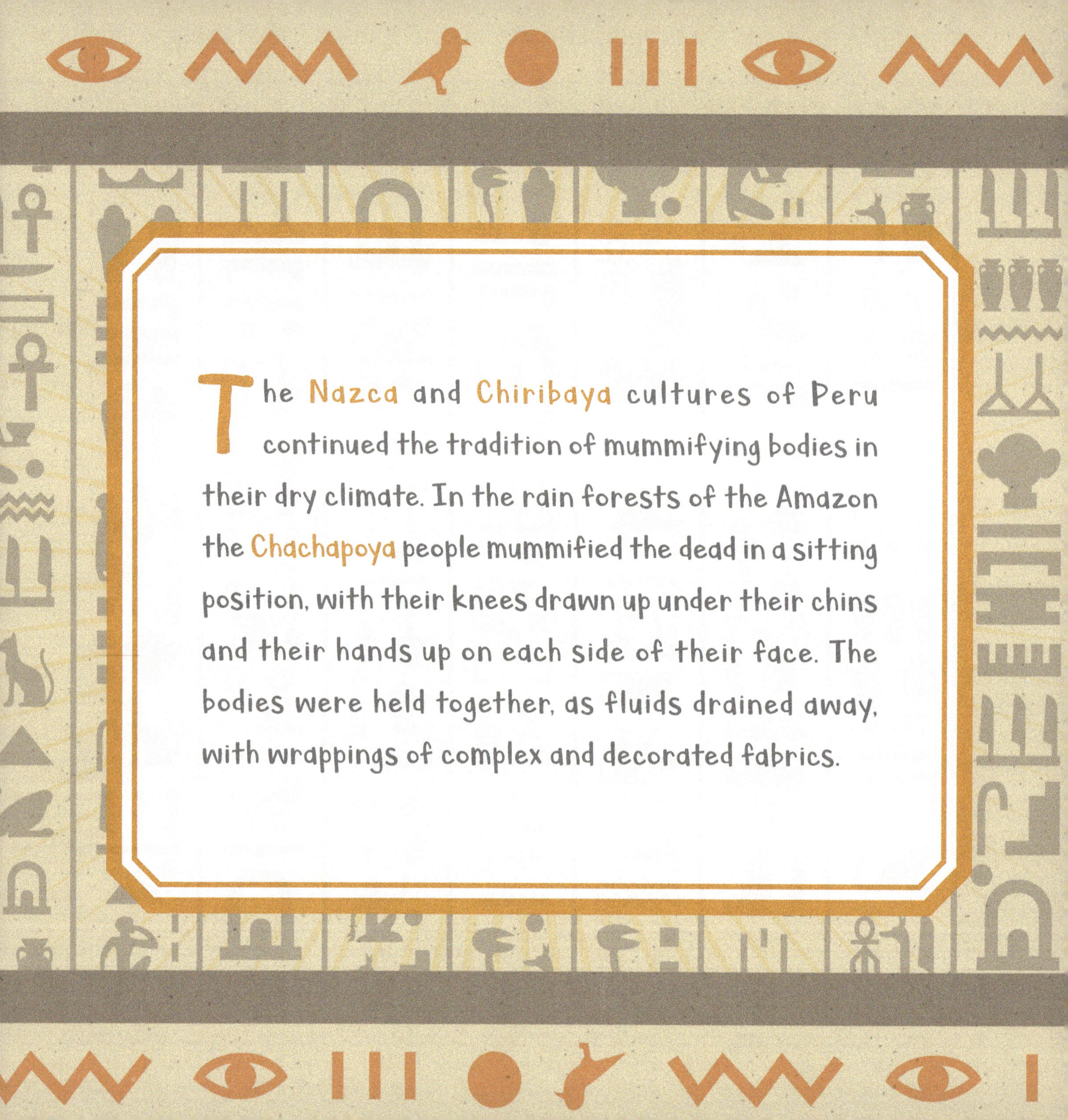

The Nazca and Chiribaya cultures of Peru continued the tradition of mummifying bodies in their dry climate. In the rain forests of the Amazon the Chachapoya people mummified the dead in a sitting position, with their knees drawn up under their chins and their hands up on each side of their face. The bodies were held together, as fluids drained away, with wrappings of complex and decorated fabrics.

CHACHAPOYA COFFIN

INCA MUMMY

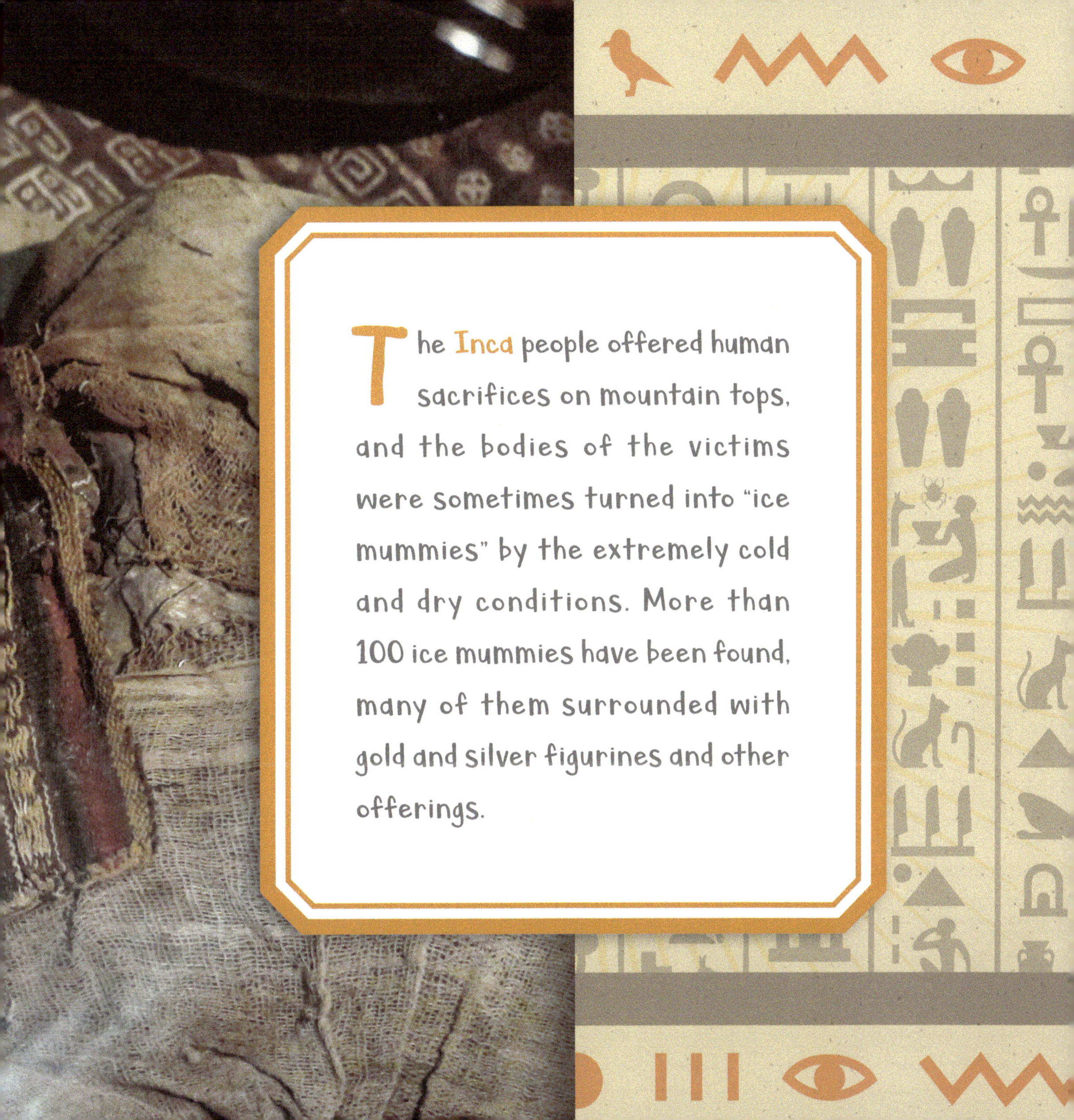

The **Inca** people offered human sacrifices on mountain tops, and the bodies of the victims were sometimes turned into "ice mummies" by the extremely cold and dry conditions. More than 100 ice mummies have been found, many of them surrounded with gold and silver figurines and other offerings.

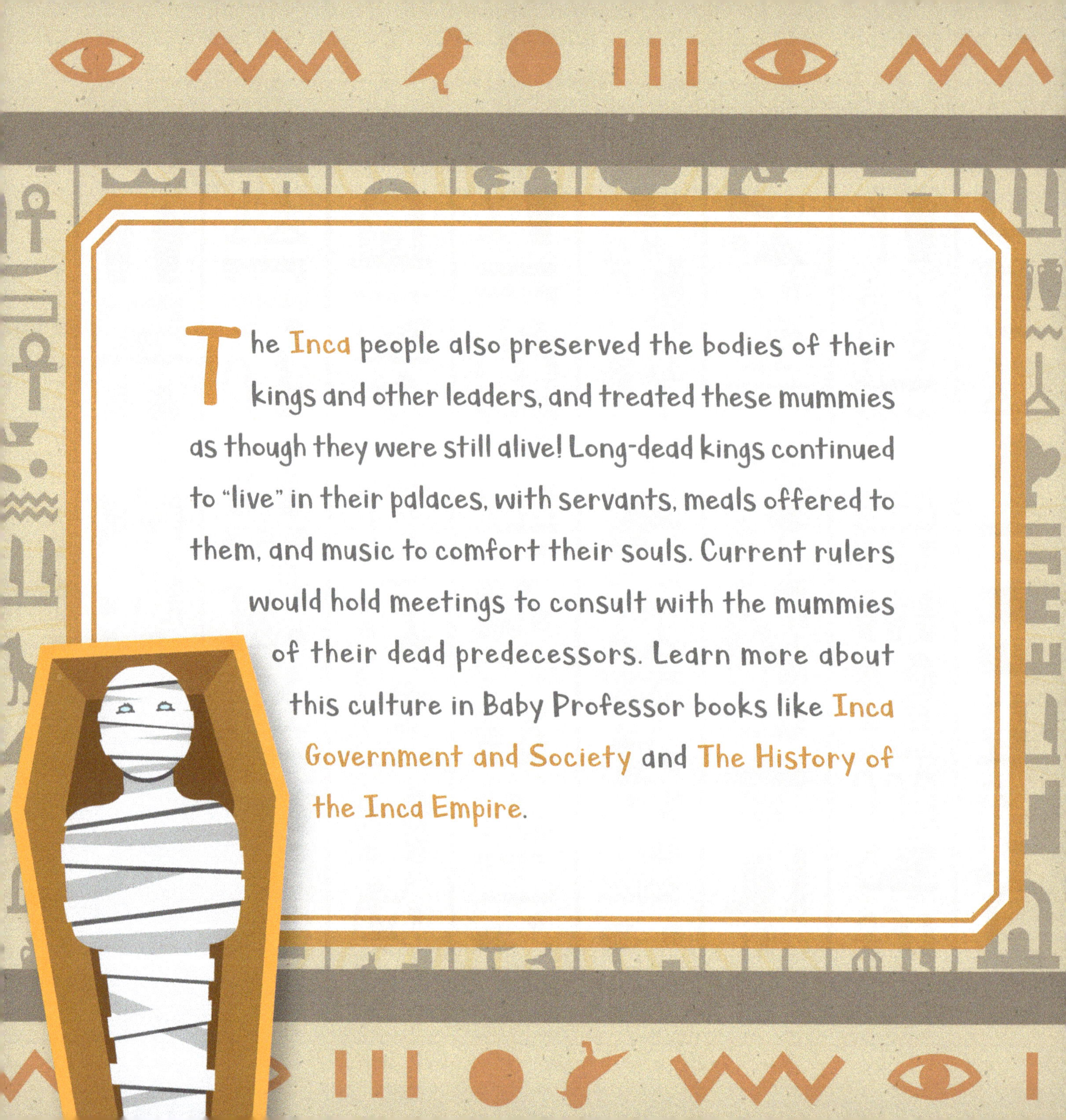

The Inca people also preserved the bodies of their kings and other leaders, and treated these mummies as though they were still alive! Long-dead kings continued to "live" in their palaces, with servants, meals offered to them, and music to comfort their souls. Current rulers would hold meetings to consult with the mummies of their dead predecessors. Learn more about this culture in Baby Professor books like *Inca Government and Society* and *The History of the Inca Empire*.

Bastar
Atahual
el inca
pa
INCA LEADER

GUANCHES

EUROPE

In Spain, the Guanches people lived in the Canary Islands, off the coast of Africa. They herded goats and lived very simply in caves, but the Guanches mummified their dead. There are some connections between their techniques and the methods the Egyptians developed, but the Guanches continued this practice until the fifteenth century CE, long after mummification ended in Egypt.

In **Northern Europe** many mummies were created more or less by accident. The Celtic peoples from about 400 BCE practiced ritual sacrifice, and would deposit the bodies of the sacrificial victims in peat bogs. The acidic liquid of the bog would preserve the body's soft tissue as a dark, leather-like material, creating "bog people".

BOG PEOPLE

TAKE A TRIP TO EGYPT

If you get a chance to visit Egypt, you can see more than mummies and tombs! Read the Baby Professor book Where Should I Go in Egypt? to start to plan your trip.